THINK

AT
CHRISTMAS

Illustrations by Julie Downing

To

Mum

with our love and

WITH BEST WISHES

FOR A

HAPPY CHRISTMAS

FROM

Julia and Michael.

1990

In the sixth month, God sent the angel Gabriel to Nazareth, a town in Galilee, to a virgin pledged to be married to a man named Joseph, a descendant of David. The virgin's name was Mary. The angel went to her and said, 'Greetings, you who are highly favoured! The Lord is with you.'

Mary was greatly troubled at his words and wondered what kind of greeting this might be. But the angel said to her, 'Do not be afraid, Mary, you have found favour with God. You will be with child and give birth to a son, and you are to give him the name Jesus. He will be great and will be called the Son of the Most High. The Lord God will give him the throne of his father David, and he will reign over the house of Jacob for ever; his kingdom will never end.'

'How will this be,' Mary asked the angel, 'since I am a virgin?'

The angel answered, 'The Holy Spirit will come upon you, and the power of the Most High will overshadow you. So the holy one to be born will be called the Son of God.'

The Gospel of Luke

chapter 1, verses 26-35

Infant holy,
Infant lowly,
For his bed a cattle stall;
Oxen lowing,
Little knowing
Christ the babe is Lord of all.
Swift are winging
Angels singing,
Nowells ringing,
Tidings bringing:
  Christ the babe is Lord of all,
  Christ the babe is Lord of all.

Flocks were sleeping,
Shepherds keeping
Vigil till the morning new
Saw the glory,
Heard the story,
Tidings of a gospel true.
Thus rejoicing,
Free from sorrow,
Praises voicing
Greet the morrow:
    Christ the babe was born for you,
    Christ the babe was born for you.

Anon (Polish)

And there were shepherds
living out in the fields near by,
keeping watch over their flocks at night.
An angel of the Lord appeared to them,
and the glory of the Lord shone around them,
and they were terrified.
But the angel said to them,

'Do not be afraid.
I bring you good news of great joy
that will be for all the people.
Today in the town of David
a Saviour has been born to you;
he is Christ the Lord.
This will be a sign to you:
You will find a baby
wrapped in strips of cloth
and lying in a manger.'

The Gospel of Luke

chapter 2, verses 8-12

Angels, from the realms of glory,
Wing your flight o'er all the earth;
Ye who sang creation's story
Now proclaim Messiah's birth:

Come and worship!
Come and worship!
Worship Christ, the new-born King.

James Montgomery

So they hurried off
and found Mary and Joseph, and the baby,
who was lying in a manger.

> The Gospel of Luke
> chapter 2, verse 16

Joy to the world! the Lord is come!
Let earth receive her King!
Let every heart prepare him room,
    And heaven and nature sing,
    and heaven and nature sing,
    and heaven, and heaven and nature sing!

Joy to the earth! the Saviour reigns!
Let men their songs employ!
While fields and floods, rocks, hills and plains
    Repeat the sounding joy,
    repeat the sounding joy,
    repeat, repeat the sounding joy.

He rules the world with truth and grace,
And makes the nations prove
The glories of his righteousness,
    The wonders of his love,
    the wonders of his love,
    the wonders, wonders of his love.

                                                  Isaac Watts

The true light
that gives light to every man
was coming into the world.

He was in the world,
and though the world was made through him,
the world did not recognize him.
He came to that which was his own,
but his own did not receive him.
Yet to all who received him,
to those who believed in his name,
he gave the right to become children of God —
children born not of natural descent,
nor of human decision or a husband's will,
but born of God.

> The Gospel of John
> chapter 1, verses 9-13

How silently, how silently,
   the wondrous gift is giv'n!
*So God imparts to human hearts
   the blessings of his heav'n.*
No ear may hear his coming;
   but in this world of sin,
*Where meek souls will receive him, still
   the dear Christ enters in.*

*O holy child of Bethlehem,
   descend to us, we pray;
Cast out our sin, and enter in,
   be born in us today.
We hear the Christmas angels
   the great glad tidings tell;
O come to us, abide with us,
   our Lord Emmanuel.*

Phillips Brooks

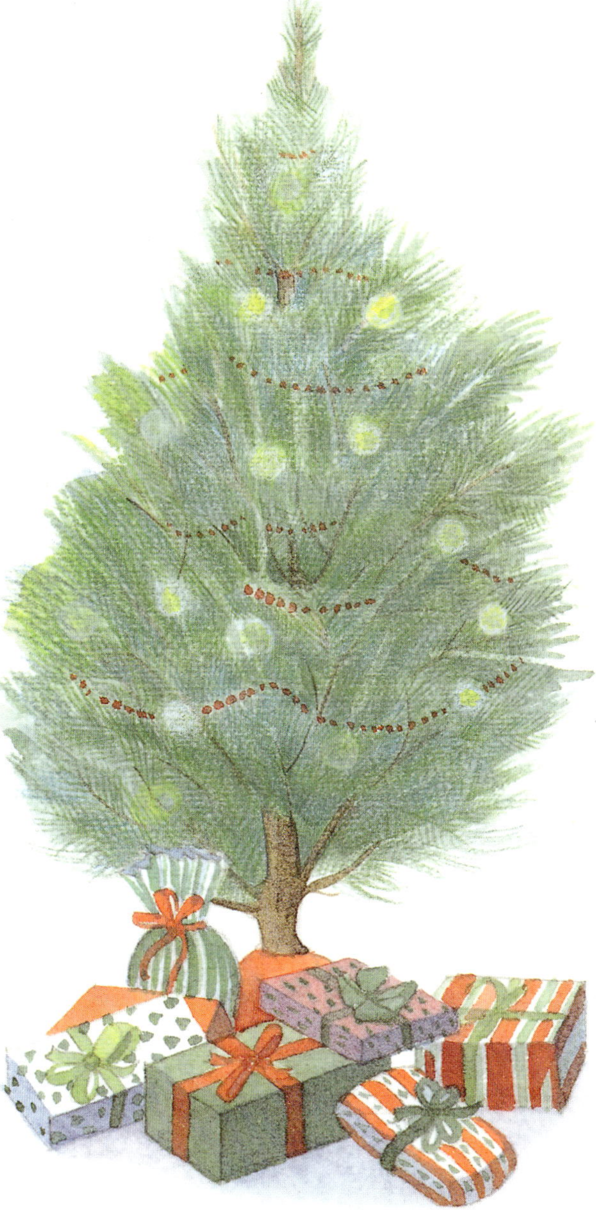

Illustrations copyright © 1989 Julie Downing
This edition copyright © 1989 Lion Publishing

Published by
Lion Publishing plc
Sandy Lane West, Littlemore, Oxford, England
ISBN 0 7459 1570 1
Lion Publishing Corporation
1705 Hubbard Avenue, Batavia, Illinois 60510, USA
ISBN 0 7459 1570 1
Albatross Books Pty Ltd
PO Box 320, Sutherland, NSW 2232, Australia
ISBN 0 7324 0013 9

First edition 1989

All rights reserved

Acknowledgments
Bible quotations from *Good News Bible*,
copyright 1966, 1971 and 1976 American Bible Society,
published by the Bible Societies/Collins, and the
Holy Bible, *New International Version* (British edition),
copyright 1978 New York International Bible Society.

Printed and bound in Italy